101 USES FOR A DEAD CUBE

BY
JOHN ZALES AND JOHN STEVENS

TOR

A TOM DOHERTY ASSOCIATES BOOK
Distributed by Pinnacle Books, New York

ISBN: 523-49013-5

Interior lettering by Ann E. Bell

A Tom Doherty Associates Original

Printed in the United States of America

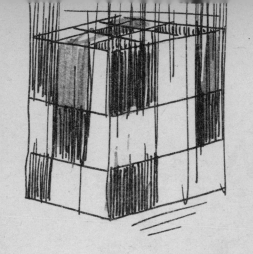

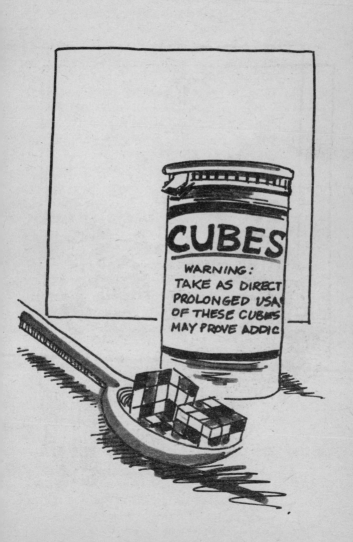

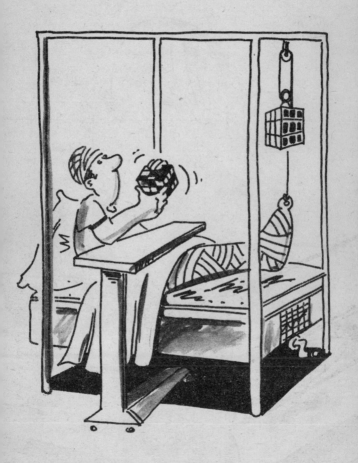